Nov, 1987

For Emilia –
        Love Aunt Jane

The
REBUS
TREASURY

Compiled by
Jean Marzollo

Illustrated and designed by
Carol Devine Carson

METHUEN CHILDREN'S BOOKS

For Martine
J.M.

For Alex and all the Devines
C.C.

*Acknowledgements and thanks to the following sources of rubber stamps: Leavenworth Jackson,
100 Proof Press, J. C. Casey, Bizarro, Mythology, Inkadinkado, and special thanks to Marty Blake.*

First published in Great Britain in 1986
by Methuen Children's Books Ltd.
11 New Fetter Lane, London EC4P 4EE
Originally published in United States in 1986
by Dial Books for Young Readers, a division of E. P. Dutton,
a division of New American Library
Text copyright © 1986 Jean Marzollo
Illustrations copyright © 1986 Carol Devine Carson
All rights reserved
Design by Carol Carson
Printed in Hong Kong by South China Printing Co.
ISBN 0 416 95530 4

Table of Contents

Introduction 5

Part One Rebus Rhymes 7
I Eat My Peas With Honey 9
Jack and Jill 10
Little Bo-Peep 11
Patty Cake 12
Mary, Mary, Quite Contrary 13
Little Miss Muffet 14
Hey, Diddle, Diddle 15
Little Boy Blue 16
The Old Woman Who Lived in a Shoe 18
Wee Willie Winkie 19
Diddle, Diddle, Dumpling 20
Ride a Cock Horse 21
Once I Saw a Little Bird 22
Hickory, Dickory, Dock! 23
Old King Cole 24
Humpty Dumpty 25
If All the World Was Apple Pie 26
Hickety, Pickety, My Black Hen 27
I Asked My Mother for Fifty Cents 28

Part Two Rebus Songs 29
Twinkle, Twinkle, Little Star 31
The Muffin Man 32
Ring-a-Ring O'Roses 33
Oh, Dear! What Can the Matter Be? 34
Lazy Mary 36
Over the River and Through the Woods 38
Eentsy Weentsy Spider 39
Jingle Bells 40
Shoo Fly 42
Pop! Goes the Weasel 43
Home on the Range 44
Red River Valley 45
Down in the Valley 46
The Riddle Song 48
The Bear Went Over the Mountain 50
Hush Little Baby 52
Lavender Blue 54
I'm a Little Teapot 56
Rock-a-Bye, Baby 57
Oh, Susanna 58
Baa, Baa, Black Sheep 60
Sing a Song of Sixpence 62

Afterword 64

Introduction

What is a rebus?
A rebus is a text in which pictures substitute for words, as in:

  U

I LOVE YOU

The rebuses in this book have been written for young children and their parents to sing and say together. A good way to go through *The Rebus Treasury* is for parents to run their finger under each line, pausing at the rebus picture and waiting for the child to "read" it. After a while the child will probably memorize most of the words to the songs and rhymes and will be able to read them on his or her own. Since rebuses are based upon the idea that symbols stand for words, they are an excellent introduction to the alphabet and reading.

Some of the rebuses used in this book are:

be   n o t   up   down   baby

dear   night   sheep   world

Part One

REBUS RHYMES

I EAT MY PEAS
WITH HONEY

 eat my  with .

 've done it all my life.

It makes the  taste funny.

But it keeps them on my .

JACK AND JILL

And broke his 👑

And 🧒 came tumbling after.

LITTLE BO-PEEP

Little  has lost her

And can't tell where 2 find them,

Leave them alone and they'll come ,

Dragging their behind them.

PATTY CAKE

Patty , patty  ,

Baker's .

Bake me a

As fast as U .

Roll it and stretch it

And mark it with a B ,

So we have

For and me.

MARY, MARY, QUITE CONTRARY

, quite contrary,

How does your 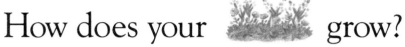 grow?

With cockle  and

And -slips all in a row.

LITTLE MISS MUFFET

Little  sat on a tuffet

Eating her curds and whey.

Along came a

Who sat beside her

And frightened  away.

HEY, DIDDLE, DIDDLE

Hey, diddle diddle

The  and the

The  jumped over the) .

The little laughed

2 C such sport

And the ran away with the .

LITTLE BOY BLUE

Little

Come blow your   .

The   's in the

The   's in the   .

But where is the

Who looks after the  ?

He's under the haystack

Fast  .

Will U wake him?

No,  .

4 if 👁 do

He'll surely 😤.

THE OLD WOMAN WHO LIVED IN A SHOE

There was an old

Who lived in a  .

She had so many

She didn't know what 2 do.

She gave them some broth

Without any  ,

Then said good-

And sent them 2  .

WEE WILLIE WINKIE

Wee [Willie Winkie] runs through the town,

[Up] stairs and [down] stairs

In his [nightgown].

Rapping at the [window],

[Crying] through the [lock].

R the [children] in their [bed]s?

4 it's past 8 o-[clock].

DIDDLE, DIDDLE, DUMPLING

Diddle, diddle, dumpling, my son

Went 2 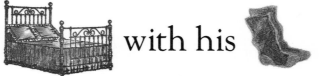 with his on,

1 off, the other  on,

Diddle, diddle, dumpling, my son .

RIDE A COCK HORSE

Ride a cock  2 Banbury Cross

2 C a fine upon a .

With on her ,

And on her ,

She shall have music wherever she goes.

ONCE I SAW A LITTLE BIRD

Once  a little

Come hop, hop, hop;

So  cried, "Little

Will U STOP STOP STOP ?"

 was going to the

2 say, "How do U do?"

But he shook his little

And far away he flew.

HICKORY, DICKORY, DOCK !

Hickory, dickory, dock,

The 🐭 ran 👆 the ⏰.

The ⏰ struck **1**,

The 🐭 ran 👇,

Hickory, dickory, dock !

OLD KING COLE

Old was a merry old soul,

And a merry old soul was he;

He called for his

And he called for his

And he called for his fiddlers 3.

Every fiddler had a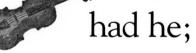

And a very fine had he;

Tweedle D, tweedle D

Went the fiddlers 3

And merry we will .

HUMPTY DUMPTY

sat on a .

had a great fall.

All the 's

And all the 's

Couldn't put together again.

25

IF ALL THE WORLD
WAS APPLE PIE

If all the 🌍 was 🥧,

And all the C was 🍾,

And all the 🌳 were 🍞 and 🧀,

What should we have 2 drink?

HICKETY, PICKETY, MY BLACK HEN

Hickety, pickety, my black hen,

She lays eggs for gentle-men;

Gentle-men come every day

To C what my black hen doth lay.

Sometimes 9 and sometimes 10,

Hickety, pickety, my black hen.

I ASKED MY MOTHER
FOR FIFTY CENTS

 asked my mother **4 50¢**

2 C the 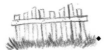 jump the .

He jumped so high

He reached the

And never came back

Till the **4**th of .

Part Two

REBUS

SONGS

TWINKLE, TWINKLE, LITTLE STAR

Twinkle, twinkle, little ,

How  wonder what **U R**

 above the so high,

Like a  in the .

Twinkle, twinkle, little ,

How wonder what **U R**.

THE MUFFIN MAN

O, do U know the

The

The

O, do U know the

That lives on DRURY LANE ?

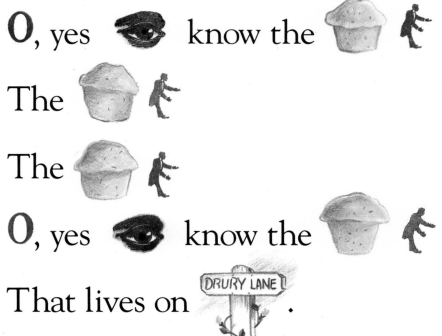

O, yes 👁 know the

The

The

O, yes 👁 know the

That lives on DRURY LANE .

RING-A-RING O' ROSES

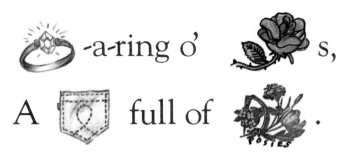 -a-ring o' s,

A full of .

Atishoo, atishoo,

We all fall .

OH, DEAR! WHAT CAN THE MATTER BE?

O  what  the matter  ?

, what  the matter  ?

O what  the matter  ?

's so long at the fair.

He promised he'd buy me a

That would please me.

And then 4 a ,

0, he vowed he would tease me,

He promised 2 buy me a bunch of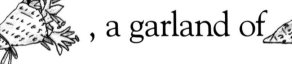

2  my bonnie 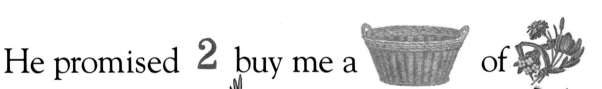.

He promised 2 buy me a  of

A garland of , a garland of ,

A little straw 2 set off the

That my bonnie .

LAZY MARY

Lazy MARY will U get 👆?

Will U get 👆?

Will U get 👆?

Lazy MARY will U get 👆?

Will U get 👆 2 -day?

No, No, Mother,

 won't get

won't get

won't get

No, No, Mother,

won't get

won't get 2-day.

OVER THE RIVER AND THROUGH THE WOODS

Over the [bird] and through the [trees]

2 [Grandmother] 's [houses] we go;

The [horse] knows the way

2 carry the [sleigh]

Through the [WHITE crayon] and drifted [snowflakes].

Over the [river] and through the [trees]

0 how the wind does [blow] !

It stings the [nose],

And bites the [foot],

As over the [bird] we go.

38

EENTSY WEENTSY SPIDER

The eentsy weentsy 🕷 went ☝ the 💦🛝 .

🧤 came the ☁🌧 and washed the 🕷 out.

Out came the ☀ and dried ☝ all the 🌧 .

And the eentsy weentsy 🕷

went ☝ the 🛝 again.

JINGLE BELLS

Dashing through the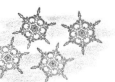

In a **1**-  open

O'er the  we go

Laughing all the way

 on bob-

Ma- 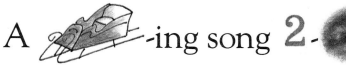 spirits bright,

What fun it is **2** ride and

A 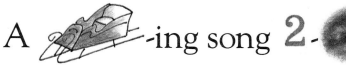 -ing song **2**- .

O jingle  jingle

Jingle all the way,

O what fun it is 2 ride

In a 1- 🐎 open

Jingle jingle

Jingle all the way,

O what fun it is 2 ride

In a 1- 🐎 open

SHOO FLY

🪰, don't bother me.

🪰, don't bother me.

🪰, don't bother me.

4 👁 🪰-long 2 somebody.

👁 feel, 👁 feel,

feel like a morning ⭐.

👁 feel, 👁 feel,

feel like a morning ⭐.

POP! GOES THE WEASEL

All around the cobbler's

The   chased the   .

The   thought 'twas all in fun,

    goes the   !

A   4 a   of thread

A   4 a   .

That's the way the   goes

    goes the   !

HOME ON THE RANGE

O give me a [home] where the [buffalo] roam,

Where the [deer] and the [antelope] play;

Where seldom is heard a discouraging word,

And the [sky] is [not] [cloud]-y all day.

[Home], [home] on the range,

Where the [deer] and the [antelope] play;

Where seldom is heard a discouraging word,

And the [sky] is [not] [cloud]-y all day.

RED RIVER VALLEY

From this valley they say **U R** going,

We will miss your bright 👁 👁 and sweet 👄,

4 they say **U R** taking the ☀ -shine

That has brightened **R** pathways awhile.

Come and sit by my side, if **U** ♥ me.

Do 〜⊗〜 hasten **2** bid me adieu,

Just remember the ✏ Valley,

And the 🤠 who ♥-d **U** so true.

DOWN IN THE VALLEY

 in the , the so low,

Hang your  over, hear the wind ,

Hear the wind , ,

Hear the wind .

Hang your over, hear the wind .

Build me a , 40 high,

So C him, as he rides by.

As he rides by, by, as he rides by,

So C him, as he rides by.

Write me a ; send it by mail

Send it in care of Birmingham .

Birmingham , ; Birmingham .

Send it in care of Birmingham .

-shine, ♥ dew,

in heaven, know 👁 ♥ U.

Know 👁 ♥ U, U, know 👁 ♥ U,

in heaven, know 👁 ♥ U.

THE RIDDLE SONG

I gave my love a cherry that had no stone,
I gave my love a chicken that had no bone,
I gave my love a story that had no end,
I gave my love a baby with no cryin'.

How can there be a cherry without a stone?
How can there be a chicken without a bone?
How can there be a story without an end?
How can there be a baby with no cryin'?

A 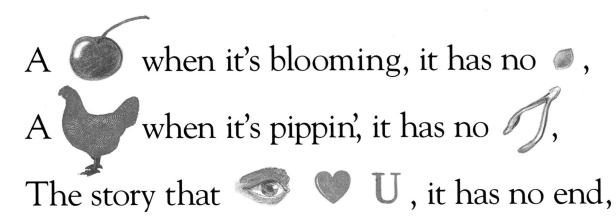 when it's blooming, it has no ,

A when it's pippin', it has no ,

The story that U , it has no end,

A when it's sleeping has no cryin'.

THE BEAR WENT OVER THE MOUNTAIN

The  went over the  ,

The  went over the  ,

The  went over the  ,

2 C what he could C .

2 C what he could C .

2 C what he could C .

The other side of the ,
The other side of the ,
The other side of the ,
Was all that he could C .

HUSH LITTLE BABY

Hush little 👶, don't say a word,

🎩PAPA 's gonna buy U a mocking 🐦.

If that mocking 🐦 don't sing,

🎩PAPA 's gonna buy U a diamond 💍.

If that diamond 💍 turns brass,

🎩PAPA 's gonna buy U a looking 🥛.

If that looking 🥛 gets broke,

🎩PAPA 's gonna buy U a billy 🐐.

If that billy 🐐 won't pull,

🎩PAPA 's gonna buy U a 🛒 and 🐂.

If that  and turn over,

's gonna buy U a named Rover.

If that named Rover won't bark,

's gonna buy U a and .

If that and fall

You'll still the sweetest little in town.

LAVENDER BLUE

Lavender's BLUE, dilly dilly,

Lavender's GREEN;

When eye am king, dilly, dilly,

U shall bee a queen;

Call 1 your men, dilly, dilly,

Set them 2 work;

Some to the plough, dilly, dilly,

Some to the cart .

Some to make hay, dilly, dilly,

Some to thresh .

While U and 👁, dilly, dilly,

Keep ourselves warm.

I'M A LITTLE TEAPOT

I'm a little ,

Short and stout;

Here is my ,

Here is my .

When 👁 get all steamed ☝,

Then 👁 shout:

Tip me over

And pour me out.

ROCK-A-BYE, BABY

Rock-a-bye,

On the top.

When the wind s

The will rock.

When the bough breaks

The will fall,

And will come ,

and all.

57

OH, SUSANNA

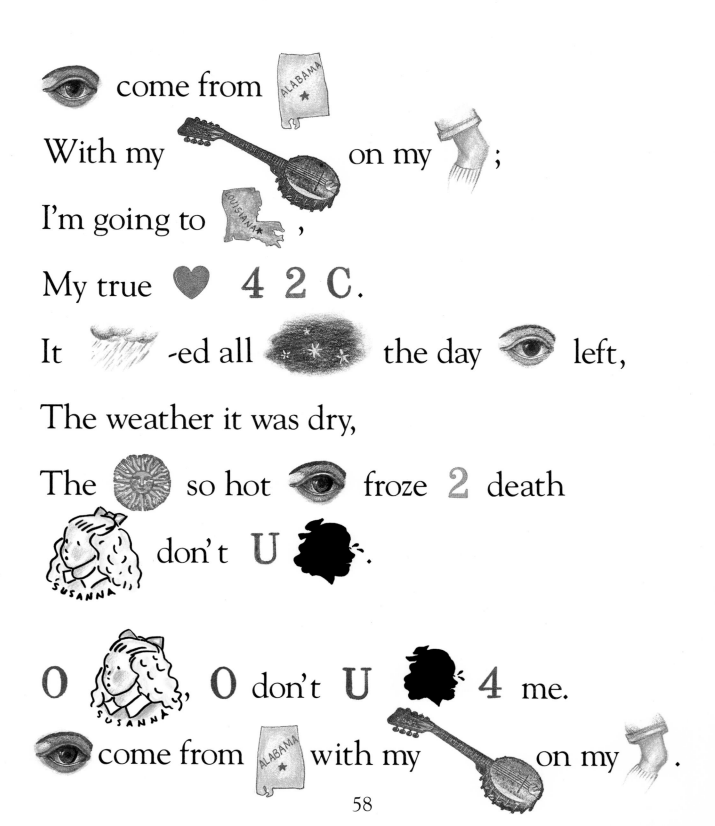

58

had a dream the other ,

When everything was still.

 thought    come

A-walking the ;

The 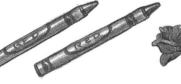  was in her ,

The was in her ,

 said, " come from

 don't U ."

BAA, BAA, BLACK SHEEP

Baa, Baa,

Have **U** any ?

Yes, sir, yes, sir,

3 full.

1 4 my master,

And 1 4 my dame,

And 1 4 the little

Who lives the lane.

Baa, Baa,

Have U any ?

Yes, sir, yes, sir,

3 full.

SING A SONG OF SIXPENCE

Sing a song of 6 pence,

A full of rye,

4 and 20

Baked in a  .

When the was opened,

The   began to sing,

Wasn't that a dainty

2 set - 4 a ?

The  was in his counting 🏠,

Counting out his 💰.

The 👑 was in the parlor

Eating 🍞 and 🍯.

The maid was in the 🌿,

Hanging out the 👕.

Along came a 🖤🐦

And nipped off her 👃.

Using pictures to stand for spoken words is an ancient practice dating back to Egyptian hieroglyphs and early Chinese pictographs, which precede the alphabet. Rebus pictures were used to convey the names of towns on Greek and Roman coins and on family seals in Europe. Later they evolved to rebus riddles, as we know them today.

The artwork in *The Rebus Treasury* is comprised of rubber stamp images and original colored pencil drawings. The stamp art is taken from nineteenth century engravings and twentieth century line drawings.